THE ABC'S OF PEO'S

A BEGINNER'S GUIDE TO PROFESSIONAL EMPLOYER ORGANIZATIONS

MARK MACKENZIE

TheABCsOfPEOs.com

This book is sold with the understanding that the author is not rendering financial, accounting, or legal services. Each scenario is unique; questions pertaining to finance, accounting, or the practice of law should be directed to the appropriate professional.

AUTHOR'S NOTE

This book is intended as a beginner's guide to Professional Employer Organizations. The hope is to make a complex topic simple, and easy to understand. It was a struggle to whittle down the topics discussed in this book to a hundred pages. It could very easily have been a couple of hundred pages. However, I wanted the reader to actually read the book, not just use it as a paperweight. Besides, you can't write a book about efficiencies and cost containment and have it be inefficient.

The subject matter is non-denominational with the sole purpose to provide objective and dispassionate insight about the benefits of a PEO partnership. The intent is not to sell the benefits of a specific PEO.

The National Association of Professional Employer Organizations (NAPEO) estimates that there are currently over 900 PEO's within the United States. Clearly one size never fits all. Measure twice, cut once, to find the PEO that is the right fit for your business.

TheABCsOfPEOs.com

CONTENTS

PART ONE – THE STATUS QUO

Chapter – 1   How Did We Get Here?   9

Chapter – 2   Demographics   15

Chapter – 3   The Benefit Dance   29

Chapter – 4   Achtung Minen   37

PART TWO – THE PEO

Chapter – 5   What Is A PEO   51

Chapter – 6   (A)ssets   71

Chapter – 7   (B)enefit Strategy   85

Chapter – 8   (C)over Your A$$ 95

Chapter – 9   Candles & The Electric Light   101

TheABCsOfPEOs.com

PART ONE
THE STATUS QUO

Chapter 1
How Did We Get Here?

"Businesses rarely come up for air to re-evaluate how they are selling. This means their current sales practices, process, and organizational structure may in fact be hindering their growth more than any external factor they believe they are facing."

Tiffani Bova

Throughout history there have been events and moments in time that have changed the course and trajectory of the economy and the world and challenged the status quo.

The invention of the telephone and the electric light. World War I. The Great Depression. World War II. The internet. And of course, the Great Recession of 2008 are all examples.

Some of these events were obviously destructive, others were constructive. But what resulted from all of them was change. There was no going back to the prior state.

So here we are in 2019, a decade removed from the Great Recession and financial crisis of 2008 and the headlines will tell you that the economy has never been better. The stock market and housing markets are at all-time highs, unemployment is near all-time lows. But beneath the surface, small business owners who are on the front lines of the economy will tell you that something or somethings have changed over the last decade, and they would be right.

Fierce competition, rising operational costs including group medical premiums, tighter profit margins, increased legislation and potential for litigation, and an anemic talent pool, have all contributed to challenges for businesses in every industry.

These economic symptoms are the product of a decade of zero or near-zero percent interest rates, trillion dollar deficits, and the Wal-Martization of America. This is our "new normal".

While the "new normal" has created a boom in financial and housing markets, the engine of the U.S economy, small business, has experienced significant head winds as GDP has struggled to maintain 2% growth since 2009.

According to the Census Bureau, the total number of actual business startups in the U.S. is at its slowest pace since 1983. Small business ownership in America this last decade has been under siege.

Shrinking Labor Force Participation

Not surprisingly, as business startups have been derailed from pre-Great Recession levels, labor force participation has also been affected. A lot of people have just dropped out of the workforce. According to the Bureau of Labor Statistics, labor force participation is currently hovering around 63% in 2019; this is the lowest rate since Jimmy Carter was in office. It's not your imagination; it is really hard to find good people to hire. And it can be even harder to keep them. In fact, at the end of the first quarter in 2019, there were approximately 1.6 million more job openings than there were unemployed workers.

It's not a coincidence that according to the National Association of Professional Employer Organizations (NAPEO), the number of PEO worksite employees has more than doubled since 2008 from 1.8 million to more than 3.7 million in 2017. The aggressive growth of the PEO industry is directly correlated to this challenging business environment.

If we have learned anything from the last decade, it's that in order to be able grow your business, profitably, you need to be able attract and retain good employees, stabilize and control your operational costs, and manage and mitigate potential liabilities.

It's one thing to grow top line revenue, but if that revenue isn't making its way through the income statement to your net operating income, all you've done is created more work and liability for yourself.

This is why the concept of a business partnering with a PEO has gained so much traction over the last decade.

Zero Percent Interest Rates

As a result of the Great Recession, the Federal Reserve has kept interest rates near zero percent for nearly a decade. While they have attempted to raise or normalize interest rates more recently, it appears that that process has about run its course. The low interest rate environment encourages the creation of debt. In our case, this free money and debt creation has allowed and encouraged companies to take on debt and acquire other companies, oftentimes their competitors. If a business can't get a return on their capital from a bank because interest rates are at or near zero, the business will chase yield by acquiring the income stream of another business entity. These types of business acquisitions and consolidations have produced the Wal-Martization of American industry.

The "Wal-Martization" of America

But it is not just Wal-Mart nor just Amazon. Large corporations in every industry across America from hospitals where babies are born to funeral homes where we are laid to rest, and every industry in between, corporations have been increasing their market share either through the acquisition or the eventual termination of smaller competitors. This trend is not likely to change as the larger these corporations become, the harder it is for small business to penetrate or maintain market share.

Longest Economic Expansion In History

Here's the good news, we are currently in the longest economic expansion in history. Here's the bad news, we are currently in the longest economic expansion in history. We don't need a PhD in economics to understand that the next slow down or recession is likely not too far off on the horizon. This means that opportunity for your business is going to come knocking soon, if it hasn't already.

Larry Bird Is Not Walking Through That Door

In 2000, Rick Pitino was the head coach of the Boston Celtics. At that time, the city of Boston, and the Celtics specifically, were in a championship drought. Larry Bird, who was revered in Boston after winning titles for Boston in 1981, 1984, and 1986, had retired after the 1991-1992 season. The Celtics had struggled in Bird's absence to find their identity and maintain their winning tradition. The fans and the media were not happy and they let Pitino know about it.

The simmering water came to a boil after the Celtics lost on a buzzer-beater to the Raptors in March of that year. Pitino unloaded during a post-game press conference, and reached internet immortality, when he said, "Larry Bird is not walking through that door, fans. Kevin McHale is not walking through that door, and Robert Parish is not walking through that door. And if you expect them to walk through that door, they're going to be gray and old. As soon as you realize those three guys are not coming through that door, the better this town will be for all of us."

Pitino's point was that this was their new reality.

The point of this book is that this is our new reality.

The next three chapters represent the specific challenges facing businesses today. How do you attract, engage, and retain good people or assets into your company? How do you contain benefit costs? And how do you cover your ass from workplace liability? For some companies, they might be struggling with just one of the three obstacles right now. For others, they might be confronted with two or even all three at the same time. However, at some point in time, every company will run up against the ABC's of business and it is how they react to them that will determine their trajectory and profitability.

Chapter 2
Demographics

"Your demographics is your destiny."

Unknown

It's not just your imagination, one of the hardest things to do as an employer is to find good people. As was mentioned in the last chapter, there are 1.6 million more job openings than there are unemployed workers. This deficit means that there is an ongoing war for talent. Employers are having to compete against one another to hire candidates, but not just any candidates.

Your Demographics Is Your Destiny

Beginning in the early 1990's the Japanese economy began its terminal decline. The symptoms of this decline manifested themselves in the stock market and the real estate market, both of which experienced jarring valuation declines.

What was once referred to as a lost decade, painfully morphed into a lost generation.

Despite unconventional and drastic monetary and fiscal policy initiatives to breathe life into their stalled economy over the last three decades, the Japanese economy is still on life support. Their GDP has had significant headwinds, unable to overcome 2% growth, while the government debt to GDP ratio has soared to over 250%. The economy has plateaued and all they have to show for it is a massive mountain of debt.

So what changed for Japan? What caused this once great economic and industrial force of nature to die a slow and painful death? Their demographics.

Japan got old. In fact, according to a 2015 Japanese census, their population actually declined in number. They hit their demographic cliff.

So what does Japan's demographic experience have to do with your business? It has everything to do with your workforce.

Your demographics is your destiny.

It is projected that by 2020 Millennials will comprise 50% of the workforce. By 2025, they will make up 75% of the labor force.

If your workforce demographics don't start to mirror these trends, your business will also hit a demographic cliff like Japan has.

It's Your People, Stupid!

In 1992, Bill Clinton, a relatively unknown governor from Arkansas, was able to defeat George H.W. Bush, a sitting President, by adopting the campaign slogan "It's the economy, stupid!" His message resonated with the American people.

To this point, it is important to never lose focus about the value that your people, your employees, provide to your business and your clients or customers.

The challenge is, how do you get the most out of your people?

What makes managing your workforce so challenging today is the fact that there are predominantly three different generations in the labor market today; Millennials, Gen X, and the Baby Boomers.

While there is some open interpretation and debate about the specific birth years that represent each generation, generally speaking, Millennials were born between the years of 1978-1995. Gen X is represented by the birth years of 1965-1977. Baby Boomers are the years between

1946-1964. Of course, these dates are not carved in stone and neither are the personalities of the individuals that were born within these time frames, but you get the point. You have people working for you that have different expectations of you and what your work culture is supposed to represent. If you are a parent of multiple children, you can probably relate to the different relationships and parenting styles you have with your children. What works with one, may not work with the other. Each employee and each child is different.

While Millennials and their uncompromising expectations have come under fire in recent years, keep in mind what Frank Martin, the men's head basketball coach of South Carolina said in 2017, "You know what makes me sick to my stomach? When I hear grown people say that kids have changed. Kids haven't changed. Kids don't know anything about anything. We've changed as adults. We demand less of kids. We expect less of kids. We make their lives easier instead of preparing them for what life is truly about. We're the ones that have changed. To blame kids is a cop-out."

The point being, Millennials represent an incredible opportunity for your workforce if you can tap into their potential by creating an attractive work experience that goes beyond a bi-weekly paycheck.

The challenge for employers is that each of these three generations have different expectations about what "work" should look and feel like. While every generation has expectations of receiving a competitive wage and benefit offering from their employer, the degree to which each generation values these items varies.

According to a 2016 engagement study conducted by ADP along with a 3rd party market research firm, MSI International, Baby Boomers weighted their compensation and benefits to represent 59% of their overall satisfaction with their employer. Meaning, so long as they are getting compensated adequately, these professionals didn't care as much about the other "stuff".

Millennials on the other hand, weighted compensation and benefits as contributing to only 44% of their overall job satisfaction.

Gen X was in the middle with a 52% weighting for compensation and benefits.

This of course begs the question, if compensation and benefits only contributes to 59%, 52%, and 44% job satisfaction for each of these generations, what the heck makes up the other 41%, 48%, and 56% respectively?

The answer is, "The Experience".

What is "The Experience"? It is all of the other stuff that contributes to employees wanting or not wanting to show up on time for work each day. And if they do show up, are they actually going to contribute to the success and profitability of the business, or are they just going to be "there".

Specifically, this stuff is not a ping pong table in your lounge or an espresso machine in your break room. And while neither of these items are in and of themselves unfavorable, depending upon your company culture, they're not going to allow you to attract, engage, and retain the best employees. Your best employees see right through these empty fads and gimmicks.

According to the study, the experience that these individuals want from their work is about company culture, things like workplace flexibility, growth and career pathing opportunities, recognition, and social responsibility.

I completely understand and respect the fact that this is not "old school", business as usual. For some businesses, these are completely new ideas and foreign concepts that they thought were reserved for companies like Apple and Google. They're not. Just as the internet shattered the status quo for how businesses marketed themselves and how we now communicate with one another, the status quo is also being shattered for how you communicate with and manage your employees.

Now here is where this conversation gets meaningful. The compensation and benefit strategy that you offer your employees are hard dollar costs. Each and every month you are writing a check for these things. And to be honest, after a while, these things begin to be taken for granted. But you probably already know this. More on this later in the book. The experience stuff, the flexibility, career pathing, recognition, etc, these are all soft dollar costs. What do these types of things really cost the business in terms of hard dollars? The answer: much less than the other stuff.

Employee Life Cycle

So where, when, and how does this "Experience" start for your candidates and employees? It starts as soon as an individual learns about your business from your web site, your job posting, Glassdoor, social media, or from one of your own employees. What do these things instantly communicate to a potential employee? As we all know, first impressions matter. And it is tough to undo a poor first impression; oftentimes you don't have a second chance. It is too easy for a candidate to find another job opportunity.

Let's play a hypothetical game, imagine I just moved to your city from a different city or state. I have a skillset that you are in need of. How do I find you or how do you find me? The clock is ticking. The longer it takes you to fill a position, the longer you have a drag on your revenue. Additionally, the longer it takes for us to find each other, the more likely I am to find your competitor or have your competitor find me.

In other words, where do you go fishing for your employees? Do you post ads on CareerBuilder or Indeed? Do you post job openings on your web site? Do you have a referral program for your employees so that they can be compensated for referring a candidate that is hired?

Is your application process paperless? If it's not, how many candidates have you lost because of it?

If your application process is paperless, does it seamlessly integrate with your applicant tracking system (ATS), your onboarding process, and ultimately your payroll, HRIS or HRMS system? Remember, you have to make it easy for the candidate to "buy" your company. If there are too many steps, redundancies, or paper involved, the fish can get loose of the hook and go back to the pond for another employer. Again, first impressions matter. The current labor market is unlike anything we have seen in the last twenty years, it is less about employees competing for jobs and more about employers competing for employees.

According to a recent Gallup survey, *State of the American Workplace* (2017), only 12% of employees strongly agree that their organization does a great job of onboarding new employees.

Are Your Employees Just "There"?

Let's be optimistic and assume you have successfully and seamlessly hired and onboarded your new employee. What happens next, how are you or your managers managing your employees? According to that same Gallup survey, only 21% of employees strongly agree that their performance is managed in a way that allows them to do outstanding work. A different study done by TLNT.com in 2015 revealed that more than half of employees reacted to a performance review by becoming disengaged or by looking for a new job.

The natural result is that if your employees are not satisfied with their manager or the management style, they check out. Employees don't necessarily leave your company; they leave one of your managers.

Taking it a step further, Gallup estimates only 33% of employees are engaged, 16% are actively disengaged. These disengaged employees, "are miserable in the workplace and destroy what the most engaged employees build." A whopping 51% of employees are estimated to be "just there", neither engaged or disengaged; they are just loitering on your premise, waiting for their next paycheck. This apathy is like poison to your culture and your business.

So what is the financial impact? Gallup estimates that actively disengaged employees cost the US between $483 billion to $605 billion each year in lost productivity. Considering GDP in 2018 was $20.5 trillion, that's 2.5%-3% of GDP. Two follow up questions, why do you have actively disengaged employees? And what are your actively disengaged employees costing your business each year?

The Iceberg

And they're gone. Finally, after mindlessly collecting a paycheck for weeks or months and eroding your culture and everything else you have worked hard to build, one of your employees decides to leave one of your managers and your company. So what? Sometimes in business, the concept of addition by subtraction has merit. Sometimes your company is better off without certain employees. Maybe it was just a bad hire. Maybe they changed. But maybe your culture or your manager created the apathy.

Employee turnover is like an iceberg.

It's what you can't see, beneath the surface that can ultimately sink a ship.

We all know the story of the Titanic, the "unsinkable" ship that struck an iceberg and sank on her maiden voyage from England to New York City on April 15th of 1912. While the iceberg is blamed for the tragedy, hubris was more likely the cause as it sped "full steam ahead" despite multiple warnings of icebergs being in the area. Compounding the tragedy was the fact that there were only enough life boats for 1/3 of its passengers.

Here is the thing about icebergs, it is estimated that only 1/10 of an iceberg's total mass can be seen above the water. So approximately 9/10th's of the mass is not visible to a ship captain nor crew member.

So how can employee turnover impact your business like an iceberg sank the Titanic?

One of the obvious scenarios is what would happen to your business and your income if one of your best employees took his or her expertise and skillset, relationships, and contacts and went to work for one of your competitors? While this may not sink your ship, it would definitely have a negative impact. This is obvious; we can see this above the surface.

However, doing a deeper dive, below the surface, what does it cost your company to source or find a new employee? How long on average does it take to fill an open position? What does this vacancy cost you or your business? How long does it take to ramp up or train a new employee? What impact does employee turnover have on the morale and productivity of the employees that stay with your company?

If you are interested, there is a web site, bonus.ly, which hosts an employee turnover calculator so as to put some context and numbers behind the financial impact of employee turnover that lies beneath the surface. Of course, depending on your industry and skillset of your workforce, some of these numbers will vary, but the fact remains that much of the cost associated with turnover is below the surface.

Aaaaaaand.........They're Gone

I don't watch South Park, but it is hard to not be familiar with the episode where Stan goes with his Dad to deposit a check from his grandma in his local bank, only to be told within seconds of depositing said check into a Money Market Mutual Fund with the bank that his money was gone. "It didn't do too well, it's gone." The episode first ran in 2009 in the heart of the Great Recession. It could easily be re-produced today from the perspective of an employer trying to hire a new candidate.

Here's a scary statistic, according to Gallup, 51% of employees say they are actively looking for a different job or watching for opportunities.

Translation, approximately half of your workforce has one foot out the door in case something better comes up. Here's another depressing Gallup statistic, 35% of employees have changed their job within the last 3 years. At that pace, what does your workforce look like in the next six or nine years? What do your customers or clients think about that?

Millennials are taking the wrecking ball to the status quo as employers find themselves competing not only with one another, but also against the "gig" economy with jobs like Uber, Lyft, Amazon Flex, Grubhub, etc.

This is just the first of three headwinds that businesses have to navigate in the "new normal" economy.

Chapter 3
The Benefit Dance

"Compound interest is the eighth wonder of the world. He who understands it, earns it, he who doesn't, pays it."

Albert Einstein

The 3 "P's" of Benefits

Understandably, the topic of medical insurance benefits has become muddied over the last several years due to government legislation and rising health care costs. What was once a simple task, has become complex.

So, let's boil it all down to the Letter of The Day, "P". Specifically, the three P's of benefits: Plans, Participation, and Premiums.

As an employer you want to offer the richest plans to your employees, Fortune 500 plans, so that you can attract and most importantly retain your best employees.

You also want to drive employee participation for those plans. It won't do you any good to offer rich medical insurance plans if your employees don't know they exist, don't understand them, or can't afford them. It also doesn't do you any good as an employer if your employee gets their benefits through their spouse. In this case, the spouse's employer is the employer of choice and that makes you very replaceable in the eyes of your employee that isn't on your benefit plan.

And finally, you want to be able to contain, stabilize, and predict premiums for those plans. If you are having difficult conversations with your employees each year about their premiums going up which is resulting in them getting smaller paychecks every couple of weeks, they will start to evaluate their employment options.

The Benefit Dance

Generally once a year, often times in the Fall, businesses embark upon a storied tradition, steeped in anxiety and uncertainty known as "The Benefit Dance". "Here we go again, how do we contain costs this year?"

Are we going to shop different brokers?

Are we going to change carriers?

What if we change the plans we offer?

Change the network?

Raise the deductible?

Offer an HSA?

Changing your oil every 3,000 miles is a good best practice. Changing your benefit plan every year as a way to contain costs isn't a great look, especially for your employees and their families that use the insurance.

Employees want consistency and security. Not only with their medical insurance plan, but also with what they have to pay for it. Unfortunately, small to mid-sized businesses are at a competitive disadvantage when it comes to offering medical insurance benefits to their employees.

So how does a small business provide consistency and cost containment to their employees with their benefit offering?

You can go out and hire a couple thousand employees, or you can partner with a PEO.

Employees Want Better Benefits

We'll start with the bad news, according to an Access Development study from 2014, 74% of employees want better benefits, and 62% would leave their current employer for better benefits. Assuming that you are paying your employees a competitive wage or salary, employee benefits are running a close second when it comes to finding and keeping the best employees.

What benefits are you offering? It's not just about medical, 401k, and PTO, things like gym memberships, tuition reimbursement, discounts programs, wellness programs, and even employee assistance programs are all becoming more prevalent, especially among higher compensated employees. Obviously you have to know the expectations for your industry.

Even if you are offering a robust benefit package, are these benefits frequently and clearly communicated, do your employees even know they exist? It is not uncommon for there to be a breakdown in communication between your employees and your human resource department about what benefits are offered.

One Size Never Fits All

In the previous chapter we identified that there were predominately three different generations in the labor market, each of which has a different expectation about their work experience and the value that they placed on compensation and benefits.

In regard to benefits specifically, one size never fits all. The challenge is to not only offer a lineup of diverse plans that will drive participation for each demographic, but just as importantly, to provide education about the plans. Open enrollment only lasts for a period of time; your employees have to live with the selections they make for 12 months. You want to make sure that your employees understand what they are signing up for so that you can properly manage their expectations for the policy year. Right or wrong, your employees will hold you accountable for the plans that you sponsor and the benefit decisions they make. You want to make sure they get it right.

The Rule of 72

The Rule of 72 is a quick formula that is used to estimate the number of years it will take for something to double in value. Generally, it is a financial equation used when calculating a projected return on your investment. For instance, if you invest $100,000 into a financial instrument that yields 8%, your investment would double in approximately 9 years. Take the number 72, divide by 8, and you get 9.

Take that same $100,000 and put it into an investment that yields 6%, your capital should double in about 12 years. Take 72, divide by 6, and you get 12. Easy enough.

Einstein is credited with saying that, "Compound interest is the eighth wonder of the world. He who understands it, earns it, he who doesn't, pays it."

In other words, interest, or the rate of increase, can be good or bad depending on which side of the equation you are on.

When you last bought a house and you were signing the paperwork at the title or escrow company you will probably recall being asked to acknowledge the loan amortization schedule which shows the total amount of interest you will pay over the life of the loan. Let's say you took out a loan for $300,000 over a 30-year term at 8% interest. The amount of interest you will pay over the life of that loan is over $490,000. Alternatively, if you obtained that same loan at just 6% interest, the total amount of interest would "only" be $350,000, a savings or delta of over $140,000 over 30-years.

For our purposes, we are going to look at the equation a bit differently as we are going to apply it to your medical insurance premium dollars that are being invested each year. Let's presume you have 50 employees and on average their monthly insurance premium is $500. The total monthly spend between you and your employees each month is $25,000 or about $300,000 per year. If your average renewal premium goes up 8% per year, assuming you aren't watering down your plans by raising your deductibles or changing networks, etc, we can safely project that in nine years your annual spend will be $600,000. Is this trajectory sustainable? Is the profitability of your company, not just top line revenue but bottom line

NOI, is that growing by more or less percent than your benefit spend is growing? Are your costs of goods sold the reason why top line revenue isn't finding its way into your bottom line? Inflation is slowly eroding your profit margins.

This hidden tax, the inflation tax, is similar to the other taxes you pay as an employer like FICA, FUTA, and SUTA. You know you are going to have to pay it. The difference is that you just don't know how much you are going to have to pay from year to year.

Much like making the minimum payment each month on a credit card balance, this trajectory is not sustainable.

When Ernest Hemingway was asked how we went bankrupt, he replied, "Two ways. Gradually, then suddenly."

Not surprisingly, you are not alone. According to a Guardian Workplace Benefits study, 8 out of 10 employers say lowering the cost of benefit administration is a top priority.

Chapter 4
Achtung Minen

"Risk comes from not knowing what you're doing."

Warren Buffett

Achtung Minen is German for Danger Mines.

While landmines have been used throughout history, dating as far back to the Civil War, they became prominent during World War II.

Landmines typically were used to defend a military position instead of soldiers. Even the mere threat of a landmine provided a powerful incentive to stay away.

Today, as a business owner, you don't have the option to stay away from the minefield; you have to be able to successfully navigate it. The following is just a brief introduction as to what lies beneath the surface.

Workers Compensation Insurance

Here are two truths about workers compensation insurance.

First, if you haven't had a claim, eventually you will. They're kind of like termites in Arizona.

Second, your workers compensation experience modification is like your credit report, once it is damaged, it takes years to rebuild it.

Admittedly, depending on your industry, workplace related injuries may or may not represent a significant risk. However, that assumes that all workers compensation claims are workplace related. That is not always the case. In fact, according to a September 2018 Research Brief by NCCI, Monday was the most common weekday for workers compensation claims to occur. Not surprisingly, Friday was the least common weekday for a claim to take place. It is not inconceivable that an employee injures themselves over the weekend and rather than seeking treatment on their own, they will fabricate a workplace injury so that they don't have to pay for the medical treatment themselves.

Whether the injury is valid or not, the larger issue is how does this injury impact your culture, what do your other employees think about the scenario? Will it impact their productivity on the job? Did you have any processes in place to prevent a workplace injury? Do you offer your employees short term disability insurance so that if they are personally injured in a non-work related accident, do they have another option to remedy the situation rather than making a fraudulent claim? Depending on your industry, do you provide weekly or monthly safety training meetings? Do you have a return to work program in place so that an injured employee can return to work with limited duties or responsibilities? Is your return to work program documented in your employee handbook? Is your handbook acknowledged by your employees? Who in your office is responsible for helping to manage your workers compensation claims? Does your current workers compensation carrier or broker even care about managing or mitigating claims; are they an advocate for you?

Employment Practices Liability

Wrongful termination, harassment, discrimination, drug testing, failure to hire, and failure to promote. These are just some of your potential employment practice hazards. Are you properly documenting your termination processes? Do you have multiple reporting channels within your company for your employees to report sexual harassment or discrimination? Are your processes consistent? Are you conducting performance reviews? Are you conducting exit interviews? What is your process for candidate interviews? Do you conduct background checks on new hires? If not, what if you unknowingly hire an employee that injures a co-worker? Are you providing sexual harassment training? Are you legally obligated to do so? What is your process for investigating a sexual harassment claim? Do you have a written policy about violence in your workplace? Could any of your processes or policies be considered discriminatory? Do you randomly drug test your employees, how about pre-hire, what about post-accident? What about medical marijuana? Do you have a process for promoting? Is this process consistent? If you have processes for these items, are they documented in your employee handbook? Have your employees acknowledged your employee handbook? When was the last time your handbook was updated and reviewed?

So why does any of this matter, obviously being on the receiving end of a lawsuit is never cheap, according to a study by Lexis Nexis in 2015, the average cost to defend a lawsuit was $125,000. But more importantly is your time. According to that same study, the average duration of an employment lawsuit was 275 days. Not surprisingly, 81% of lawsuits ultimately result in no payment. But the damage has already been done to you and your company.

Group Medical Insurance

While offering group medical insurance may not necessarily be at the top of your liability list, here are a couple of perspectives on the topic.

First, the easiest thing to do as an employer is to give your employees a benefit. The hardest thing to do as an employer is to take that benefit away. When you look up the word "liability", one of the definitions is "an obligation". If as an employer you choose to offer your employees benefits, and as this book details, there are a lot of good reasons to do so as benefits have a multiplier effect, you want to make sure you can continue to do so that you don't have to take it away at a later date. It is a lot harder to undo a mistake than to get it right the first time.

Second, in regard to the concept of being self-insured or self-funded. While there are benefits to this type of solution, there is also risk and liability. What is the maximum potential exposure you have as an employer? What would happen to the company if that was realized? Do you have stop-loss insurance?

Third, speaking of maximum exposure, how much are your employees on the hook for in regard to their maximum out of pocket with a fully insured plan? Do they know what this amount is? Are they comfortable with this amount? What would happen to them if this amount was realized? How would that impact their employment and attitude towards your company?

Fourth, what about medical insurance premium cost containment from year to year? Now that you are sponsoring a group health plan, how confident are you in your ability to contain and stabilize those costs for your company and your employees each year? Is your workforce getting any younger? What happens if one of your employees gets sick and has a shock loss? What do you do if you get an unfavorable renewal with your broker? Do you change brokers, change carriers, change plans? How do your employees perceive these changes?

401(k)

Offering a 401(k) plan is a great way for an employer to add another cost effective benefit for their employees. Like most benefits, you have options. Do you want to offer just a traditional 401(k) plan? Do you want to offer a match? What type of match do you want to offer? What about a safe harbor match? What about profit sharing? What type of profit sharing; pro-rata, new comparability, age-weighted? What do you want your vesting schedule to be? What about a Roth option?

One size never fits all, and depending on your objective, you can tailor the answers to these questions so as to develop a cohesive strategy.

However, with every reward comes an element of risk.

There are two ways to get into hot water with your 401(k) plan, timely contributions and fund selections.

The Department of Labor requires that the employer deposit deferrals as soon as possible, but no later than the 15th business day of the following month. Clearly most employers want to be compliant and to stay out of the purview of the Department of Labor and the IRS. The potential for the violation or the breakdown in timely deferrals is generally a symptom of a deficient administrative process more than it is an intentional act. Regardless, the exposure is there if your payroll and 401(k) providers are not integrated.

The second potential for liability comes in the form of fund selection. What funds are you going to make available to your employees within your company sponsored 401(k) plan? You don't want to make these decisions as nothing good will come from your decision, only liability.

Specifically, there are two designations of fiduciary liability associated with 401(k) plans, they are 3(21) and 3(38) fiduciary. As we will reveal later in the book, one will provide you protection, the other will unnecessarily expose you to risk.

Government Alphabet Soup

Depending on your employee threshold, there are different levels and layers of state and federal government compliance that need to be tended to so as to keep the alphabet agencies at bay. Acronyms like ACA, COBRA, DOL,

FLSA, FMLA, EEOC, OSHA, and the DHS represent just some of the mines that litter the landscape.

The following few paragraphs are a cursory overview of the alphabet soup and are not to be taken as scripture.

While the individual mandate was repealed in 2019, the Affordable Care Act, ACA, is still alive and well along with the reporting and form 1095.

The Consolidated Omnibus Budget Reconciliation Act, COBRA, requires employers of 20 or more employees to provide workers who lose their health benefits the opportunity to continue their group health coverage.

The Fair Labor Standards Act, FLSA, is responsible for employee wage protection in regard to minimum wage, overtime, and exempt employee classifications. Are all of your employees classed correctly in regard to exempt and non-exempt?

According to a January of 2013 New York Times article, U.S. Secretary of Labor, Hilda Solis, the "new sheriff in town", was credited with collecting over $280 million in back pay as a result of over 250 investigators being added to the Department of Labor's Wage and Hour Division.

The Family Medical Leave Act, FMLA, requires employers of 50 or more employees to provide their employees up to

12 weeks of unpaid leave during any 12-month period for the purposes of a health condition, newborn child, or adoption.

The Equal Employment Opportunity Commission, EEOC, is charged with enforcing laws prohibiting job discrimination. This can apply to your job posting, your job description, your interview process and the questions you ask, your performance management and promotion standards, and ultimately your termination process. Are you asking the same questions of every candidate? Are you properly training your employees? What is your process for promoting an employee? What is your process for performance reviews? How about terminating an employee? As recently as 2017, the EEOC now has a website scheduling system for individuals to submit an inquiry online about their employer.

The Occupational Safety & Health Administration, OSHA, is tasked with overseeing that employers are providing standardized and safe working conditions for their employees. To this point, they have the power to levy penalties to employers that don't meet these standards and in 2016, these penalties were "modernized" due to not keeping pace with inflation over the years. Hazardous materials, safety training, head protection, ladders, lifts, and wiring are just a few of the exposures they can and will investigate.

The Department of Homeland Security, DHS, and more specifically, Immigration & Customs Enforcement, ICE, has the authority to audit your I-9 forms. As recently as 2018, ICE stated that they served over 5,200 audit notices across the country. Are you using the most up to date I-9 form? How long are you keeping these forms on file for? Are they held in a separate file? Do you have the proper supporting documentation?

Again, this is just a high-level assessment of the mine field.

We just listed of no less than a dozen potential liability exposures for your business as it pertains to your workforce. And we're not even doing a deep dive yet into the weeds. Depending on the maturity and experience of your business, the trigger events for these liabilities oftentimes will be met with an "ad hoc" reception. A frantic, inefficient, and desperate scramble to avoid an inevitable and painful outcome.

You would probably agree from personal experience that it is a lot harder to undo a mistake than to get it right the first time.

How many times have you made a purchase and allowed the lower price of a product or service to be your deciding factor?

And the follow up question, how many times after making this purchase have you had to correct the mistake of the initial purchase with another purchase of the item or service you should have bought in the first place?

So instead of being in it for "x", you are now in it for "x" plus "$" as well as all of the time that you wasted along the way trying to save a buck.

There is a better way.

As a reminder, the purpose of this book is to introduce a complex concept in a simple way. There's a reason why the cover has children's multi-colored building blocks on it and it is only about 100 pagers long. This chapter is just a high level, 30,000-foot view of the battle field, I mean business environment, which we find ourselves swimming in.

Navigating and demining the playing field is best done proactively rather than reactively.

Achtung Minen.

PART TWO – THE PEO

Chapter 5
What is a PEO?

"If you can't explain what you are doing as a process, you don't know what you are doing."

William Edwards Deming

We'll get to "What is a PEO" in a minute as there is a lot to unpack on the topic, but first, a bit of history.

The date was August 6th of 1945; the Enola Gay had just dropped an atomic bomb on Hiroshima, Japan. Three days later, Nagasaki was devastated by another atomic bomb. Six days later Japan surrendered to the Allies. The war was over. But the rebuilding had not yet begun.

So how could a country on a small island in the Pacific that was on the receiving end of not one, but two atomic bombs, recover so quickly and reinvent itself so efficiently into a manufacturing power house and the second largest economy in the world within just a few years?

Enter William Edwards Deming. Deming was sent to Japan in an effort to facilitate the reconstruction due to his expertise as an engineer and statistician. Specifically, his focus was on improving the quality of product and process. Deming's experience was that by focusing on incremental quality improvements, expenses would actually decrease, and productivity and revenue would increase.

In Deming's book, *Out of the Crisis*, he details his philosophy on quality and it can be simplified into one equation:

Quality = Results / Costs

He believed that quality was a function of results and costs. When companies focus on quality, costs tend to decrease over time.

When companies focus on costs, specifically on cutting costs, costs tend to actually rise because quality will decline.

Fortunately for the Japanese, in the aftermath of the war, they didn't have an army of bureaucrats in Washington DC aiming to "compliance" them into submission with regulation, reporting, and regret. The focus was on rebuilding.

The Japanese were able to focus on their core competencies. Manufacturing widgets.

Unfortunately, businesses in America today don't have this same freedom that existed 60-70 years ago as was detailed in Chapter 4. As a result, entire industries like payroll and human resource providers have been born so as to alleviate the administrative burden from small businesses.

Three Options

Two principals that have had staying power throughout time are, first, the person or the business with the most options at their disposal typically "wins". And second, only having one of "anything" is dangerous. If you have two, you have one. And if you have one, you have none.

If you have ever played the game Rummikub you have experienced this firsthand. Rummikub is game that is characterized by individual tiles with a different colored number on them from 1-13. The goal is to make "melds" or sequences with these tiles either by color or number. The sequences are either a straight of the same color, or a three of a kind with different colors of the same number. The first person to use all of their tiles in the different melds is the winner. Typically the individual that is able to identify the most meld options with their tiles will win the game. With one exception. There are two wild card tiles that can be used to complete any meld or potential meld. The individual that holds a wild card has more options and is at a competitive advantage, than the player that doesn't possess a wild card. And that is where things get really interesting with game strategy.

So what does Rummikub have to do with your business and PEO? PEO is the wild card solution. Most businesses are only looking at two options for the infrastructure trajectory of their business.

First option, the "status quo". Under this option, the presumption is that you currently have the people and the processes in place, the infrastructure, to accomplish your strategic goals. Oftentimes this "infrastructure" is an owner wearing multiple hats and or a controller or CFO, with little human resource experience, also assuming the role of the Director of Human Resources. For a company with a larger footprint, perhaps you have the people with the proper expertise on your staff already. Regardless, the status quo means that you don't want to make any changes in regard to your infrastructure, your people, or how you manage liability and contain your operational costs.

The second option is going out to the labor market (the same labor market where there are currently more than 1.6 million more job openings than there are unemployed workers), posting an ad on a web site, and interviewing multiple candidates to fill your newly created position to handle the administrative responsibilities of the business for things like payroll, HR, benefits, and managing safety and liability. If this is the plan, the question that you need to ask is, will this person be a good fit for your culture? Will your culture be a good fit for this person? You can make a good hire but if your culture is bad, they won't stick. Or you can make a bad hire and they can ruin your good culture. How much do you need to pay them? What is the cost of payroll taxes on top of that wage? What about the benefits that you need to provide to him or her? Will they contribute to the profitability of the company? Or will your revenue per employee metric be negatively impacted by them? Bringing on a new employee carries risks and costs.

The third option that a lot of business owners don't recognize, despite it hiding in plain sight, is the Rummikub wild card, the PEO partnership. The PEO partnership provides scale and infrastructure regardless of footprint or headcount trajectory. Not surprisingly, this is the option that gives the highest probability of winning.

Enter The PEO

Nobody ever went into business so they can "do" HR, payroll, workers compensation insurance, and administer medical insurance benefits. That's not why you do what you do; it's not in your DNA. But because you are in business, all of these things need to be done and done efficiently and consistently if you are to maintain a profitable business.

PEO is the offloading or outsourcing of the non-income producing activities of the business.

PEO is everything you ever wanted, but never knew existed.

PEO is an acronym that stands for a Professional Employer Organization. I also like the term "Proactive Employer Organization" or "Productive Employer Organization" as we'll discuss later in the book.

In reality, it is a partnership between a business and the Professional Employer Organization that results in a co-employment relationship in regard to your employees. In general terms, the business retains the asset, the income producing, widget manufacturing, and service providing employee. The business gets all of the "good" things associated with having employees including the interviewing, the hiring, the firing, and everything in between. The PEO gets all of the payroll, HR, and benefit administration responsibilities along with the workplace liability. In other words, all of the "bad" things associated with having employees.

Four Puzzle Pieces

Specifically, there are four puzzle pieces to this co-employment partnership between a business and the PEO. First, the PEO processes payroll and withholds the appropriate payroll taxes. Second, they provide human resource infrastructure and best practices. Third, the PEO provides workers compensation insurance. And fourth, they provide and administer group benefit programs.

The business still maintains sovereignty of its day to day operations and management decisions. The employees are still your employees.

Depending on the needs of the business, some of these puzzle pieces may be larger than others. For example, maybe containing costs with workers compensation is a primary need. For others, maybe it is administering a cost-effective benefit plan. Maybe for another business it is the payroll and human resource infrastructure. Regardless of the different sized puzzle pieces, all four of them fit together seamlessly.

Not Employee Leasing

What a PEO isn't is an employee leasing relationship.

There are essentially four ways to maintain a workforce. Picture a bell curve distribution graph. On the left side of the graph, you can do everything yourself. On the other far end of the spectrum, you can have a staffing company do most everything for you in the form of employee leasing where a 3rd party provides your company with their employees typically on a project-specific or temporary basis. In the middle of that spectrum is the PEO partnership. Finally, somewhere between doing it yourself on the left, and the PEO in the middle, is what is called ASO, or an Administrative Services Offering. The ASO solution provides payroll and human resource infrastructure, but it does not specifically address the other two pieces of the puzzle which are workers compensation insurance nor benefit cost containment. Nor does an ASO allow for shared workplace liability. An ASO can provide perspective and insight, but when the rubber meets the road, it is not going to insulate your business from risk. Clearly one size or solution never fits all, there's a reason why employers make the decisions they make. However, for the purposes of this book our focus is on why the PEO solution provides the most economically viable solution for most businesses.

Underwriting

One consideration worth mentioning about the co-employment and the PEO partnership is that it does necessitate an underwriting process. This is not just a simple vendor relationship. It is an integrated partnership of shared responsibility and liability with many moving parts and exposures. Because of this, not every company or applicant will be accepted into every PEO. Depending on the financial and credit worthiness of your business, the health experience of your workforce, and the loss history of your workers compensation policy, it is possible that a PEO won't find the partnership to be an equitable venture.

In order to determine if the partnership has the potential to be equitable, PEO's have an underwriting process, not dissimilar to a life insurance or mortgage application, that allows them to determine risk. This process will include the review of your current and prior benefit information, financial information, your workers compensation policy and loss runs, an employee census, and any number of questions about employment practices and potential risks associated with your business.

It is a lot of information. But remember, more energy is spent during the first few minutes of the liftoff of a space shuttle than will be expended during the entire journey.

If every business were approved or accepted by a PEO, it would undermine the value proposition of the PEO and its ability to save money and contain costs in regard to medical insurance benefits and workers compensation.

So now that we have unpacked the small stuff, we can move onto the more important details.

Is vs Does

Here is an exercise for you. Take a blank piece of paper and put your company name in the middle and circle it.

Now, draw a line from that circle and write in the name of your current payroll provider or the name of the person within your company that handles your payroll if you don't outsource that function.

Now draw another line from your company name in the center and put in the provider or the person that handles your human resource functions.

What about another bubble for your time and attendance solution for your employees?

Go ahead and draw another line from your company name in the center and put in the name of the company that handles your workers compensation insurance.

Let's draw another line from the center for the company that handles your major medical insurance benefits, maybe it's your broker.

What about another bubble for your dental or disability insurance contacts?

Draw another line from the center with the company that handles your 401(k). Sometimes there can be a couple of different bubbles or contacts here with a broker, a third-party administrator (TPA), and the provider.

What about another bubble for Employment Practices Liability Insurance?

And another bubble for recruiting or your Applicant Tracking System?

How about another bubble for your Employee Assistance Program?

At the end of this exercise you should have an illustration with multiple bubble extensions or entities that you are currently doing business with. These are all of your "people" vendors.

Here are some questions. How many of these vendors are integrated and communicating with one another and with you? How many different invoices are you receiving each month from these companies? Does your recruiting and onboarding system speak to your payroll and HR system? Does your payroll system speak to your workers compensation policy? Does your payroll system speak to your 401(k) plan? What about payroll deductions for medical benefits and benefit reconciliation? How many people do you need to notify when an employee is terminated?

How about your employees, how easily do they make changes to their tax withholdings and 401(k) deductions? What about benefit elections? What about clocking in and out? What if they need a pay stub or W-2? What about asking for time off? Do they have their own employee portal, or are they asking you or your office staff for all of these things?

Now draw a line connecting each one of these exterior bubbles or vendors to one another. This is what a PEO infrastructure will do for you. It will consolidate all of your stand-alone vendor contracts into one efficient partnership, minimize redundancies and waste, and create operational efficiencies,

The Quarterback

While all of this automation and integration is wonderful, what separates the PEO solution from just a technology solution is the people, specifically, the human resource business partner or specialist that is dedicated to support your business.

Technology is fantastic, but if there is low utilization, there is little benefit to even the most robust platform.

Think about a smart phone. Smart phones provide incredible potential but the majority of users only utilize a small fraction of the functions like texting, taking pictures or videos, and of course the Facebook app.

What if I told you there are approximately 2 million apps available at the Apple App Store. Obviously nobody has the time to evaluate the efficacy for each and every app. But what if there were an app store expert whose only job was to partner with other like-minded individuals such as yourself and to intimately understand your personal goals, challenges, processes, and habits, and could instantly provide you a tailored app solution that would save you time and money on the things you already do every day or every week. Since time and money are two things that we all have a limited supply of, this type of solution would probably have value to you.

Now keep in mind, this app store expert is not replacing your partner or your spouse or your current controller or Human Resource staff, nobody is getting fired or divorced, all they are doing is identifying areas of opportunity to save you time and money. Most people would not be offended by this solution.

Unfortunately, too often, companies invest in a payroll or a Human Resource Information System (HRIS) or a Human Resource Management System (HRMS) and they are left alone to figure out how to get the most efficient utilization out of the platform.

Think of a private airplane. A private plane can take you anywhere in the world and it can do it much faster and more efficient than any other form of travel. Here is the challenge though. If the captain were to simply toss you the "keys" to the plane, how far do you think you would get? Not very far. You need a captain, a first officer, a mechanic, and maybe a flight attendant for safety (or medical benefit open enrollment). You get the point. A plane in and of itself is impotent without the properly trained and experienced crew. This is the challenge with a technology-only solution for your payroll and human resource administration processes.

However, when you have the right people in the right places to fly the plane, an interesting thing happens, you begin to slowly get your company bandwidth back.

Reallocate

If you have kids, or if you can remember back to watching Sesame Street as a kid, you will likely recall the segment of the show known as the "Word of the Day". It's when Elmo and or Cookie Monster introduce a new word to the audience.

Here's our "Word of the Day": Reallocate.

According to the Merriam-Webster dictionary, reallocate means to:

a: to apportion or distribute (something) in a new or different way b: to earmark or designate (something) for a new or different purpose

Currently your business is allocating a certain number of hours towards processing payroll, benefit administration or reconciliation, or any number of other human resource tasks. According to a 2015 HR World survey, 80% of an HR department's time was spent on paperwork and administration. None of these activities yield a real return nor actually produce any income for the business. But these things still need to be done.

What if these tasks could be offloaded or automated and you were able to reallocate this time, money, and energy towards improving your company culture, training, coaching, career development or career pathing your employees, improving the quality of your service or product, maybe even launching a new service or product.

Initiatives like career pathing don't have to be complicated. Use the KISS principle, Keep It Simple Stupid. For example, hire new employees as an "associate". After a probationary period of time or a certain level of accomplishment, maybe three to six or nine months, they achieve a different title like "partner", or whatever you want to call it. Maybe that new title also provides a small bump in pay, better parking spot, more PTO, better hours, more responsibility, additional cross-training, whatever.

You know your business and employees better than I do. Then maybe the next promotion is to "senior" or "magician" or "warlock" or "sorcerer" or whatever you want to call it. You get the point, it's your company, and it's your culture. You can make it fun, or not, entirely up to you. Maybe get feedback and buy-in from your current employees and let them help design their own career path. And like everything else, document it, make it part of your handbook, promote and communicate about it, often. This is not intended to make more work for you, it's intended to enhance the work experience, improve engagement, and decrease turnover.

Career pathing, career development, along with trainings, and other initiatives all have the potential to positively impact your profitability. In other words, instead of allocating hours to work "in" your business, those hours were reallocated to work "on" your business.

The people you currently have doing administrative functions obviously are good people, otherwise you wouldn't have hired them. The question is whether you are truly leveraging their valuable and unique skillsets that would contribute most to your success?

Improved Communication

The offspring of the PEO partnership, the opportunity to reallocate time and dollars, results in improved communication throughout your company. And not just any communication, but the medium and the frequency of communication. One size never fits all. How many times have we seen or personally experienced the lines of communication breakdown in businesses and families because there is a deficit in the frequency or the method of communication?

Or has communication broken down because everybody is too busy doing their job that they forget about the bigger picture.

The "Why?"

Do your employees know why they do what they do? Do your employees even know what the bigger picture even is? Not to get philosophical, but do you know why you do what you do? Is there even a bigger picture?

Wildly Important Goal

In Franklin Covey's *4 Disciplines of Execution* (4DX) management program, they discuss the WIG, or the Wildly Important Goal for a business. Specifically, identifying what that one goal is, communicating that goal throughout every division and employee of your company, and accomplishing that goal in the face of distractions and competing priorities. Decreasing the administrative burden and improving communication allows you to narrow your focus. "Focus on less to accomplish more."

Mitigation

Now that we have automated, integrated, and reallocated, the last step is mitigation. Finally, going back to the bubble illustration, draw one big circle around all of the smaller circles on the paper. This is what a PEO "Is". A PEO is the integration and automation of all of these moving parts and pieces. But it is also more than that. The outer circle also represents an additional layer of insulation for the business from the workplace liability that is associated with all of these parts and pieces. There is additional protection for you, the employer when these functions are aggregated through a co-employment partnership.

If you have ever watched the national geographic channel you are probably familiar with the scene where a herd of buffalo is carefully navigating their way through the African plains. After some peaceful videography, the British narrator announces the arrival of the lion pride that is quietly staking their positions so as to test the herd and identify weak spots or vulnerabilities. So long as the buffalo herd stays together, they are safe. The moment that they become divided or separated from one another, chaos ensues, a plume of dust is kicked up, visibility becomes limited, and all hell breaks loose. The challenge for a business is to keep the pack, their people and their processes, together and out of harm's way.

So now we know what a PEO "Is", the next three chapters are going to dive into what it actually "Does".

Chapter 6
(A)ssets

"If you challenge conventional wisdom, you will find ways to do things much better than they are currently done."

Bill James

How Do You Intend To Grow Your Business?

Conventional wisdom says there are three ways to grow your business. You can grow by employee head count, you can increase the productivity of your current workforce, or you can introduce a new widget to the marketplace. Maybe it is some combination of all three.

In regards to the first two, increasing headcount and or increasing the productivity of your workforce. How do you intend to accomplish this?

Why would a qualified candidate come to work for your business rather than one of your competitors?

Why would one of your current employees spontaneously increase their output or productivity for you or one of your managers?

TheABCsOfPEOs.com

Who is your best employee? Why are they your best employee? I realize it is a bit like asking you who your favorite child is. But what would happen to your profitability if they left, what would happen to your profitability if you could find another one or two just like them? These questions, and the related answers, all fall into the genre of Human Capital Management.

Human Capital Management

Let's face it; finding quality, competent, and committed employees is tougher than a $2 steak. Like curing cancer, no treatment plan is 100% effective, but some do have higher success rates than others. Success leaves clues. The latest trendy corporate buzzword word, Human Capital Management, or HCM, refers to the process of how companies effectively acquire, manage, and retain their employees. In other words, where do you go "fishing" for your best employees and what "bait" do you use? Do you have an employee referral program? How do you get them onboarded and into your boat? Once you have a new employee how do you get them to work really hard for you and maintain their peak performance? And how do you not tick them off so that they want to leave your company? While each of these touch points are independent of one another, together they form a continuous process known as the employee life cycle which was discussed in more detail earlier in the book. For the purpose of this chapter and in order to avoid redundancy, we are going to focus on the meat of the topic, employee engagement which correlates very closely with productivity.

Employee Engagement

We used the term, Proactive Employer Organization previously. We could also use the term, Productive Employer Organization. According to the National Association of Professional Employer Organizations, companies that partner with a PEO grow 7-9% faster than their counterparts. Employee engagement is a big part of this and admittedly it is part art and part science. But there are a couple of truths with nearly every employee in every industry. Marcus Buckingham, the founder of the Marcus Buckingham Company, is recognized as a leader on Talent. Specifically, on how to increase performance in the workplace. Marcus states, "We do things at work because they are useful, right. So the question with the performance review is what is it for?" His opinion is that they are not immediate enough nor necessarily actionable. They are inherently reactive. Instead, performance reviews need to be more frequent and proactive. What's next, what's around the corner, how do we prepare ourselves for the next steps? Think coaching not managing. How are you coaching to get the maximum productivity and effectiveness out of your workforce?

"What Gets Measured, Gets Managed"

"Continental Airlines, in early 1994 was going nowhere, and it was going nowhere fast. If you wanted to get anywhere else fast, like New York or Denver or Cleveland- or, in fact, if you wanted to get anywhere at all and get there on time-you were better off flaying almost any other airline. But nowhere? We were going nowhere like we had an appointment. And nowhere is where we could get you, though we probably would have lost your luggage along the way." (Bethune & Huler *From Worst To First – Behind The Scenes of Continental's Remarkable Comeback,* 1998)

So how did Gordon Bethune, the Former Chairman and CEO of Continental Airlines transform the "Washington Generals" of the airline industry to a two-time winner of the J.D. Power Award for customer satisfaction and being named the Airline of the Year by *Air Transport World*?

They began by measuring the right things, the right way.

To this point Bethune states, "Businesses fail because they want the right things but measure the wrong things-or they measure the right things in the wrong way, so they get the wrong results."

Moneyball

Over the last 25 years baseball has morphed from a sports industry into a data analytics industry. Franchises have invested millions of dollars in the accumulation, mining, study, and application of statistical data so as to leverage predictive analytics.

The statistical revolution that first began in fringe, small market franchises like the Oakland Athletics with their general manager Billy Beane and his obsession with a metric known as on base percentage, has morphed into a game that is hardly recognizable to traditional baseball fans. The explosion in the number of strikeouts and homeruns, the lost art of the stolen base, the disappearance of the sacrifice bunt, the slow extinction of the triple, "the shift", "the opener", launch angle, and the left-handed specialist out of the bullpen are all products of baseball's stat-heads. All of these changes were the result of how teams began to measure and manage the performance of their players. As a result, the modern form of baseball has become highly efficient, there is very little waste. Every pitch, every swing, every out is heavily scrutinized so as to achieve maximum yield or production out of the opportunity.

Not surprisingly, it also changed how teams valued their players. Statistics that once had tremendous value, like being a .300 hitter, have lost value if that hitter doesn't have any power or can't earn a walk. On the other hand, a player that bats .225 with 150 strikeouts, but has power, has more value than he would have had 25 years ago.

Perhaps what is just as fascinating about the statistical revolution in baseball is the impetus that lead to it. The Oakland Athletics are a small market team. In any given year, Oakland had a payroll that was at most 1/2, sometimes 1/3 that of the larger market teams in their league like the New York Yankees or the Boston Red Sox. The Athletics were at a competitive disadvantage to the rest of the league. Yet they were still tasked with competing against these teams that could spend millions more than they could.

Necessity is the mother of invention. Oakland had to get real efficient with how they allocated their capital. They couldn't afford to go out to the market and sign a 40-home run guy, but they could go out and sign a guy that got on base .40% of the time. So that is what they did.

Despite winning 103 games in 2002, and 20 in a row at one point during that season, winning a World Series has proved elusive for Beane and his team. Critics will cite this as evidence that his concept of Moneyball is a failure. The reality is Moneyball has been a wild success, so much so that 29 other franchises have implemented "Stat-head" divisions within their front offices, filled with Ivy League statistic majors, that have adopted and evolved the concepts that Beane revolutionized which has resulted in even more fierce competition for Oakland as their attempt to pull away from the peloton has been thwarted. The Athletics have been swallowed up by their peers who began using their same statistics and strategies.

So what metrics are you using to measure your workforce productivity?

A reasonable baseline indicator is to measure your revenue divided by the number of your employees. Take a look back over the last few years and see what this ratio looks like. What about your NOI divided by the number of your employees? Is there a trend?

What about your HR cost per employee?

Diving a little deeper, how long does it take for you to fill an open position? What is this vacancy costing the business?

What percentage of your job offers are accepted? How much time and money are you losing because a candidate chooses another company over yours?

What is your voluntary and involuntary termination rate for the year? How much is that costing your company?

These are all great metrics that can be measured and managed, so long as you have the bandwidth to do so.

"What gets measured, gets managed."

Positive Arbitrage & The Extra 2%

Here's the reality, chances are that your business is already highly efficient. It has to be otherwise you wouldn't still be in business. These metrics and analytics are not necessarily about making wholesale changes to your business processes. It's about the extra 2%.

The Tampa Bay Devil Rays were a baseball expansion team that made their debut in 1998. Their first decade in baseball created a legacy of losing as they lost more than 90 games each and every year. A few years they were exceptionally awful and lost over 100 games. They were very consistently a very bad team. However, in 2005, two former Goldman Sachs bankers acquired the team and brought with them a Wall St. concept of positive arbitrage.

Positive arbitrage is the simultaneous buying and selling of a security for a small, but risk free profit. Although rare, an arbitrage opportunity may temporarily present itself in foreign exchange markets or different stock exchanges where an investor can buy a currency or a stock in one market and quickly sell that same currency or stock for a small profit in another market. However, as financial markets, much like baseball, have become highly efficient over the years, these types of arbitrage opportunities have become more rare.

However, in the mid 2000's there was still arbitrage opportunities in baseball and the new Devil Rays owners exploited it. In Jonah Keri's book, *The Extra 2%,* he details how the former Goldman Sachs colleagues did two things really well, arbitrage and cost containment.

Specifically, in regard to arbitrage, the new Devil Rays owners identified defense as a metric that was undervalued by the league. Every other team was focused on offensive statistics and metrics, but not much attention was being paid to the other half of the game, the defense. And so that is where they began to focus their attention. Amazingly, from 2007 to 2008, the Devil Rays went from worst to first in the American League East, not an insignificant accomplishment considering Boston and New York, teams with the largest payrolls in baseball, were also in that division. Tampa Bay went from a 66-96 record in 2007 to 97-65 the following year. Not by accident, they went from allowing 944 runs in 2007, to just 671 in 2008. Amazingly, the Rays made it to the World Series in 2008 only to be defeated by the Phillies.

The other thing Tampa Bay started focusing on was cost containment. Specifically, adding club options to contracts that were signed on their younger players. They knew they wouldn't be able to keep these players for the long term because teams like the Yankees and Red Sox would simply out spend them. The Rays had to find a way to contain and stabilize costs of their players and they accomplished this through adding club options onto their contracts.

The point of these baseball stories is that competition yields opportunity. There is always another way to become more efficient, overcome obstacles, and succeed.

Becoming An Employer of Choice

Remember from earlier in the book we discussed how millennials would make up 75% of the workforce by 2025.

Where do millennials want to work?

They want to work at companies like Google and Apple and Microsoft and Intel, just to name a few.

What do these companies have in common besides the obvious that they are technology or software companies that satisfy their employees' need for digital? They are also really good at delivering a positive work "experience" starting from the application process, to the onboarding process, to career development and growth opportunities, to job flexibility, and recognition and every step in between.

Obviously these companies have economies of scale and infrastructure and resources that you don't have. They are publicly traded companies. They have highly compensated employees. They may be operating in different industries than you are. This is all true. But it doesn't mean small businesses can't mirror their best practices.

What is Zappos Doing That You're Not?

Zappos is an online shoe and clothing retailer. The company is not exactly in the mold of being a Silicon Valley technology darling. They're actually based out of the desert in Las Vegas, Nevada, not Silicon Valley. And yes, while they were acquired by Amazon in 2009, we have to ask ourselves "why" did Amazon acquire this online shoe and clothing retailer instead of just putting them out of business. Doesn't Amazon eat companies like this for breakfast?

In 2013 Zappos received 31,000 applications for 350 job openings. That's nearly 90 job applications for one job opening...... for an online shoe retailer. Understandably this large volume of applicants provides its own set of challenges, but again, it's nice to have options. Obviously Zappos is doing something different than what most other retailers and businesses are doing. So what are they doing differently? They have embraced technology and social media, but not just at a corporate and pre-packaged level, their employees have become ambassadors and the face of the company. Zappos employees have blended their work life with their personal life. Zappos is so confident in their company culture that they encourage their employees to connect with, promote, and provide outstanding service to their customers outside of the corporate biosphere. They trust their employees.

Zappos, an online shoe retailer, has become an employer of choice because they have succeeded at providing a superior work "Experience" to their employees.

Customer Branding vs Employee Branding

Every company is aware of the importance of their "brand" as it pertains to their customers. They understand if their brand is damaged, or non-existent, that it will negatively impact their market share and their profitability. Companies spend thousands of dollars a year branding themselves in media and online, and it works.

What some of these companies have begun to realize is that employees are "consumers" of the workplace. They can either buy in and become engaged and advocate for your company and help you attract good employees, or they can check out. By buying in and becoming engaged, employees are more likely to be productive and subsequently, profitable. So how do you know how to brand your company to your employees? Ask them. Have you considered putting together a branding club or a culture club? A small group of your employees, elected by their peers, can responsible for developing the culture and the internal brand of your company. And if you have successfully implemented something like this and you have developed internal advocates for your company, have you ever considered leveraging this advocacy and compensating your employees for referring new employees into your company?

Your employees are assets, and if untethered, are capable of doing amazing things for your company.

Tactical HR versus Strategic HR

Maybe you are already doing all of these things and you are pitching a perfect game with your employees. But maybe this chapter has also peeled back the curtain to new opportunities for you to engage with and get the most out of your employees. This transformation is from tactical human resources to strategic human resources.

Tactical human resources is making sure your company is in compliance with the latest I-9 form and that you store all of your I-9s in a separate file. It's updating your employee handbook to reflect new PTO legislation. Tactical is all of the administrative work that has to be done that adds very little value to the organization or your employees.

Strategic human resources is all of the stuff that impacts the engagement, retention, and productivity of your employees.

A PEO partnership removes the tactical HR burden from your staff so that you can invest your time and resources into strategic HR and getting the most out of your people.

Chapter 7
(B)enefits Strategy

"If you do what you have always done, you'll get what you've always gotten."

Anthony Robbins

Earlier in the book, in Chapter 3, we discussed the three "P's" of a comprehensive benefit strategy. Offering the best plans, driving employee participation, and containing premiums. This is great and all, but how do we actually do this. Like with everything else in business, the devil is in the details.

Let The Ball Be Your Feedback

In case you didn't know by now, I love baseball. I can't get enough of it. So here is another baseball anecdote. Joey Votto plays first base for the Cincinnati Reds. You could make the argument that he has been one of the most efficient hitters in baseball over the last ten years. Incredibly, he's lead the league in on base percentage seven times in his career. In a recent interview he was asked how he has been so consistently successful for so long, his answer was, "let the ball be your feedback."

Regardless of your hitting mechanics, the ball is going to tell you what you did right or wrong with each swing. If you pulled the ball or popped it up, if it had backspin or topspin, the ball will tell you what you did right or wrong with your swing.

To this point, what are your benefit results telling you about your current benefit strategy? Are you offering rich plans that your employees actually want? Are your employees enrolling in and actually using your plans, if not, why not? Are you able to contain and stabilize the premiums of your plans for your employees? What feedback, verbal or non-verbal, are your employees giving you about the benefits that you provide? Your employees are the "consumer" of your benefit strategy.

The Multiplier Effect

There are instances in business where the sum is greater than the parts. Employee benefits are one of those instances. It has a multiplier effect. Providing your employees with rich medical plans and a 401(k) plan, and even better, contributing generously to these plans, allows you better compete for top talent. The more talented and dedicated employees you have working for you, the more profitable your company will be. If executed properly, your benefit strategy will yield more than the investment that you made in it.

Fortune 500 Benefits

Why do the best employees want to work at Fortune 500 companies? Part of it is prestige, part of it is security, another part is the experience, but make no mistake, a big part is the benefits. According to Talent Culture (2015), 57% of employees would be willing to accept a job with lower compensation but a better benefits package. It's no secret, large companies can offer better benefits at a better price than small companies can. So how do small companies compete with Fortune 500 companies? How do teams like the Oakland Athletics and Tampa Bay Rays compete with the Boston Red Sox and the New York Yankees? They do things differently. Rather than hire a few thousand employees, you can partner with a PEO that has a few thousand worksite employees.

A PEO gives your company economies of scale and buying power. More importantly, it provides insulation, cost containment, and predictability moving forward.

Cost Containment

The projection on the following page illustrates the potential cost savings of a medical insurance renewal that compounds at 6% vs 8% based on an initial $300,000 annual premium spend. Over a 4-year period, the savings would equate to over $68,000. Of course, if the delta between your current benefit strategy and that of a PEO is more than 2% per year the savings would be greater. Additionally, the further out you project, the more the savings would be. This illustration was intended to provide a very conservative example about how just a small change or decrease in a medical insurance renewal rate or premium can have a profound impact as it is compounded year over year.

	Proj Increase	Year 1	Year 2	Year 3	Year 4	Year 5		
Current	8%	$ 300,000	$ 324,000	$ 349,920	$ 377,914	$ 408,147	$	1,759,980
PEO	6%	$ 300,000	$ 318,000	$ 337,080	$ 357,305	$ 378,743	$	1,691,128

Total Savings $ 68,852

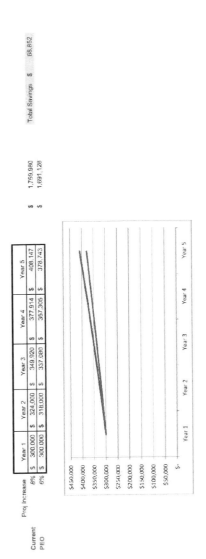

TheABCsOfPEOs.com

The next projection shows a 6% annual compounded renewal compared to a 10% compounded renewal over a period of four years for a projected savings of over $140,000. We could provide illustrations all day long; perhaps one year you have a dreadful renewal in excess of 18% because one of your employees got sick. How would you absorb that? Ultimately there is not a crystal ball but the one thing for certain is that the cost of medical care will continue to rise indefinitely. As a result, medical insurance premiums will also rise. One of the best ways to mitigate this risk is to further insulate your business by leveraging the economies of scale of a PEO.

Total Savings $ 140,402

$ 1,831,530
$ 1,691,128

	Proj Increase	Year 1	Year 2	Year 3	Year 4	Year 5
Current	10%	$ 300,000	$ 330,000	$ 363,000	$ 399,300	$ 439,230
PEO	6%	$ 300,000	$ 318,000	$ 337,080	$ 357,305	$ 378,743

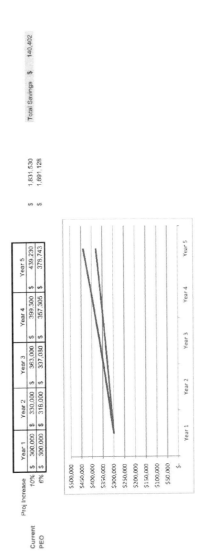

When Is The Best Time To Buy Life Insurance?

In the insurance industry there is a term for people and companies that are considered to have an elevated risk; it's called "adverse selection". Essentially what this means is that those that want or need the insurance the most, are also at the highest risk of utilization of that insurance. Insurance companies don't like this. Insurance companies don't like risk. There's a reason they have been around for over 100 years and their names are on top of high rises in cities all across the country. They don't want to insure people that are going to use their product.

For example, life insurance is predominately sold proactively, meaning there is a sales agent or a broker that is soliciting the sale of the insurance product from a healthy applicant. In rare instances, an individual will react to a recent health scare or diagnosis and attempt to procure life insurance. This application will be met with the hawkish eyes of an underwriter and *if* approved, the insurance company will be compensated with elevated premiums in order to offset the increased risk or adverse selection. There is no free lunch for the insured. In many instances, the insurer will even decline coverage entirely because there is simply too much risk.

So when is the best time to apply for life insurance? When you are young and healthy.

When is the best time to partner with a PEO for medical insurance savings and cost containment? When your group is young and healthy.

The fuse has been lit, the reality is that for every individual you employee, and for every year that goes by, your group health insurance rates are a business liability waiting to be exposed.

Total Compensation Statement

Finally, wrapping it up and putting a bow on this chapter, a total compensation statement is a gentle reminder to your employees that you are doing much more for them than just a paycheck. It is a report that illustrates and aggregates all of the benefits that your company provides to them. Benefits like major medical, an HSA or FSA, 401(k), paid time off, disability insurance, life insurance, dental insurance, vision insurance, cell phone reimbursement or discounts, maybe even educational assistance or reimbursement programs.

If you are doing these things for your employees, you need to be able to consistently communicate this value to your workforce. At a minimum, an annual performance review would seem like an appropriate opportunity for this type of communication. If you are not doing some of these things, you may not to reconsider your benefit strategy.

Chapter 8
(C)over Your A$$

"Most of us spend too much time on what is urgent and not enough time on what is important."

Stephen R. Covey

Proactive Employer Organization

Earlier in the book we made mention of a Professional Employer Organization being more appropriately termed a Proactive Employer Organization, and it is true. Being a proactive employer as it pertains to employee engagement, containing benefit costs, and managing liability is what will allow you to maintain a predictable income stream for your business.

While PEO's are not omniscient, they do provide perspective that can only be earned through experience. When it comes to identifying best practices, or potential pitfalls or blind spots, PEO's are uniquely qualified due to their scope of business. They are an aggregator of experiences across diverse industries. They're not unlike a coach. The best coaches in sports are generally the ones that have had the most repetitions and experience at something. They have learned, the hard way, what to do, and more importantly, what not to do.

In Malcolm Gladwell's book, *Outliers,* he makes an observation suggesting that anyone can become an expert in anything with 10,000 hours of experience or work. PEO's have this type of experience, and more, and can provide a unique perspective because of it.

To this point, this lends itself to the concept of being proactive. It's nearly impossible to be proactive if you don't know what you don't know or you don't have the bandwidth to act on what you do know.

Keeping Up Is Easier Than Catching Up

Naturally, being proactive dovetails into "keeping up". If you have ever tried to lose weight, or to reach a predetermined financial goal, you will appreciate the fact that it is unsettling when you have to play "catch up". It's a lot harder to catch up than to keep up because you have to sacrifice more energy, time, or money now than you are probably comfortable with. What's harder to do, lose 50 pounds over the next year, or to maintain a healthy weight year round? The concept of "keeping up" applies to many different areas of managing risk associated with having employees.

Clearing A Minefield

Hypothetically speaking of course, let's say you are out for a walk and you stumble upon a yellow and black sign with a skull and crossbones that is staked into the ground that says "Danger Mines". If you are like most people, you are likely going to freeze in your current state and not take another step. Now, let's presume there is a person walking next to you that calmly pulls out a map that clearly illustrates the way forward out of the minefield. This person says, "Don't worry, I was here just last week, follow me, and I'll get us out of here."

Two good things ae happening here. First, this person has clearly been here before and has a roadmap to get you out of harm's way. Second, this person has volunteered to go first.

Everything new is difficult.

The easiest way to navigate or demine a minefield is to have somebody else do it for you.

In Chapter 4 we detailed the minefield landscape, from workers compensation, to your medical insurance benefits, to 401(k), and the alphabet soup of government compliance with things like ACA, COBRA, DOL, FLSA, FMLA, EEOC, OSHA, and the DHS. We're not going to rehash the nuances of each and every exposure but the takeaway is that a PEO can provide additional insulation for your business either through the implementation of proper risk management, employee pooling in the case of benefits, 3(38) fiduciary protection for your 401(k) so that you are not making fund lineup decisions, employment practices liability insurance, or even numerous human resource or safety trainings.

When Building A Castle, Dig A Moat First

Your business represents tens of thousands of hours of your time and energy. You've invested hard earned capital into starting and growing your company. Dozens, if not hundreds of employees, and their families, depend on your ability to keep the doors open and their paychecks arriving on time. You've built your castle. Have you also dug a moat?

Successful People Don't Take Risks

There is a term that you are probably familiar with; it is called "risk tolerance". The term is commonly used in the financial planning industry to begin a conversation about investing and your time horizon. The thought is that if you have a long time before your retirement, you should have a higher risk tolerance and be able to take on more risk. And there is some truth to this. But what if you don't need a return on your investment, what if you only need a return of your investment? In other words, what if you are simply trying to preserve what you have.

As a business owner you have something that not many other people have, you have what every investor wants, you have a stream of income. You don't need the stock market to go up every year in order to retire, nor do you need to sell your stocks to support your retirement. You already have your business and all of the future income that it represents to you, your family, or a potential buyer when the time is right.

You are not in the business of taking excessive risks anymore. You already did that when you started your business. Now, you are in the business of preserving and protecting what you have built.

Chapter 9
Candles & The Electric Light

"The electric light did not come from the continuous improvement of candles."

Oren Harari

Throughout history, "Eureka Moments" have represented turning points and provided the impetus for change. Some man, or some women, after having been wronged for the last time has said, "Enough of this, there has to be a better way".

In fact, this may very well be the reason you started your business in the first place. There was an agitation or a disappointment or frustration and you saw an opportunity, you acted on it, and you never looked back.

Maybe it's the reason you decided to buy this book.

One of the more notable turning points in human history of this type of eureka moment was the evolution from candles to the incandescent light bulb. I use the term evolution lightly because candles didn't evolve into a light bulb; there was a paradigm shift, a platform change. In the beginning, the candle and the bulb both provided a similar benefit to the owner; however the objects were very dissimilar. Over time, the candle became obsolete and the incandescent light bulb evolved into the highly energy efficient, long lasting, and cost effective LED bulb that we use today. Think payroll service as the candle and a Professional Employer Organization as an LED.

The late professor and author Oren Harari, illustrated this concept when he said, "the electric light did not come from the continuous improvement of candles." Thomas Edison, along with numerous other like-minded innovators, changed the way that illumination was delivered to society. They didn't use the same "tried and tested" roadmap for candle manufacturing. They burned that blueprint and forged ahead with an entirely different solution. And it worked.

Henry Ford is known to have said, "If I had asked people what they wanted, they'd have told me a faster horse".

Rip Off The Band-Aid

So what is the point? I'm an advocate of properly managing expectations; we are talking about a workplace disruption. A PEO partnership is not just business as usual, there are too many different moving parts and pieces. If it were business as usual, it wouldn't have much of an impact. My best advice is to "rip off the Band-Aid". In other words, lean into and embrace the changes you are going to make.

Things don't have to be broken in order for you to fix or improve them. What you are doing now probably works just fine. Your current payroll solution "works". Your current health insurance broker "works". You may not have any pain. More often than not, the businesses that choose PEO are not broken or dysfunctional. They don't live on the Island of Misfit Toys. Not at all. The businesses that choose PEO are proactive businesses that are in search of the extra 2%, they are always looking at ways to get better, to innovate, to become more efficient, to simplify, to compete, to become best in class so as to attract the best employees. They are healthcare providers, manufactures, auto repair shops, HVAC companies, banks, dentists, architects, and technology companies, to name just a few. These businesses realize that if they are not improving, their competitors are. If you have employees, and they have value to you and your customers or clients, then a PEO will have value to you.

Winning In Business

How do you define winning in business? If we were to ask 10 different business owners we would get 10 different answers. Some of them would be business related, others might be more personal. And they would all be right. Everybody has a different "why". However, in order to achieve that "why" certain things need to fall into place. Things like attracting and keeping good employees to produce income for your business. Stabilizing costs as it pertains to your workforce with benefits, workers compensation insurance and unemployment insurance. Offloading and mitigating as much liability and worry as possible. And finally, freeing up the administrative burden and allowing you and your employees to focus on your core competencies, which is the reason you got into business in the first place.

At the core of all of this is maintaining a predictable and stable stream of income while detaching yourself from the red tape that has become interwoven into today's business climate.

Predictable Income Stream

What does a PEO have to do with your income stream? In a word, everything. PEO's help you to thread the needle. They help you to maximize the ROI that you are currently making in your workforce every month while minimizing the risk associated with that same workforce and all of those moving parts. Your people produce sales, provide services, manufacture products, and are on the front lines of your business with your customers and clients. PEO's free you up from the weekly whirlwind so that you can focus on your people and your culture and the PEO can focus on containing costs with medical benefits, workers compensation insurance, SUTA, managing liability, and driving operational efficiencies.

An Expense vs An Investment

If a financial planner or advisor ever approached you about an investment that would yield a predictable and stable income stream, would you consider this income stream to be an expense or an investment?

By definition, if capital yields a return, it would be considered an investment.

Yet, some business owners still myopically look at PEO as an expense. Rather than focusing on the quality of their product and their people, some businesses are still in the business of finding ways to cut costs. As William Edwards Deming illustrated, cutting costs has the potential to negatively impact the quality of your product or service, and subsequently your profits.

A PEO partnership is an investment in your company and your people. Just as you have invested capital in a web site, and a telephone system, or an advertising or marketing campaign, you made these investments because you expected them to yield a return. The investment that you make in a PEO is an investment in the quality of your company which will over time lower your operational expenses and subsequently improve the profitability of your company. The price is what you pay; the value is what you get.

Quality = Results / Costs

PEO's help you to get to where you want to go a little faster, more profitably, and with less risk.

Why partner with a PEO? Because it works.

ABOUT THE AUTHOR

Mark MacKenzie draws upon a decade of combined experience in human resource outsourcing, employee benefit strategies, and business risk management to provide PEO services to small and medium-sized businesses.

He currently resides in Phoenix, Arizona with his wife Sarah and their six children; Jackson, Carter, Madison, Grant, Lincoln, and Ford.

Made in the USA
Columbia, SC
06 July 2022